EMERGENCY!

A LEGO® ADVENTURE IN THE REAL WORLD

Did you notice that "ambulance" is spelled backward? It's so drivers can read it in the mirror.

■SCHOLASTIC

New York   Toronto   London   Auckland
Sydney   Mexico City   New Delhi   Hong Kong

Welcome, LEGO fans!

LEGO® minifigures show you the world in a unique nonfiction program.

This leveled reader is part of a program of LEGO® nonfiction books, with something for all the family, at every age and stage. LEGO nonfiction books have amazing facts, beautiful real-world photos, and minifigures everywhere, leading the fun and discovery.

To find out about the books in the program, visit www.scholastic.com.

Leveled readers from Scholastic are designed to support your child's efforts to learn how to read at every age and stage.

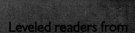

1 LEVEL READER
Beginning reader
Preschool–Grade 1
Sight words
Words to sound out
Simple sentences

2 LEVEL READER
Developing reader
Grades 1–2
New vocabulary
Longer sentences

3 LEVEL READER
Growing reader
Grades 1–3
Reading for inspiration and information

Contents

4   Emergency!

6   Fire!

12   Call the police!

18   Ocean heroes

20   Hospital heroes

26   Mountain rescue

30   To the rescue!

32   Index

BUILD IT!

Check out the epic building ideas when you see me!

Got an emergency? We're on it.

Find out about the hometown heroes who help in this book. Let's go!

Emergency!

Help! Emergency! Call 911 and an emergency team will leap into action. Off they go! They zoom to the rescue, no matter where you are. On land, in the air, even at sea, they are ready to help. Find out about some awesome heroes and the amazing jobs they do every day. Let's go!

Firefighters are always ready to help. They work as a team. One hero is great, but a whole team of them is AWESOME!

The coolest part of a rescue team? The vehicles! Find out about them inside.

BUILD IT!

Build an emergency vehicle. How fast will it speed to the rescue?

The police make sure everyone follows the rules. Make sure YOU don't speed through this book!

I'm awesome, but the everyday heroes who help are the REAL superstars.

Fire!

Make way! Lights flashing and sirens screaming, the fire truck speeds to the rescue. Fires can spread fast, so fire trucks need to get there quickly. The firefighters use long hoses to spray water on the flames. Nozzles at the end of the hose help control the jets of water.

Did you know that dogs have been part of the fire station crew for more than three hundred years?

Woof, woof!

Big fires need plenty of water to put them out. Special tanker fire trucks can carry over 1000 gallons (3,785 liters) of water. That's enough water to fill 47 bathtubs. This fire will be out in no time!

Oh no! The hoses can't reach this fire. No problem—
call in the ladder truck! Some fire trucks carry giant
ladders to reach tall buildings. The firefighter climbs
onto a platform, then WHOOSH! The ladder
stretches up toward the building.
The ladder may reach as high as
100 feet (30.5 m). That's as
high as 762 minifigures
standing on top of
each other.

Firefighters
usually work a 24-hour
shift. They cook, sleep,
and do chores at
the station.

When an
emergency call comes in,
they take action, even if
it is dinnertime!

Help! That poor guy's cape is on fire. Call the fire department immediately!

Stop! It's just my fiery fashion sense. Now my cape is all wet!

BUILD IT!

Build a very tall building. Then build a very long ladder that can reach the top!

Help! A wildfire is burning out of control! Wildfires are super dangerous. They can spread at nearly 15 miles per hour (24 km/h), destroying everything in their path. This is no job for a regular fire engine. Bring on the fire plane and its brave pilots! The largest planes can dump 12,000 gallons (54,553 liters) of water onto the flames.

HEARD THIS WORD?

wildfire: A large and dangerous fire that burns out of control in a forest or grassland area.

Call the police!

Uh-oh, someone has broken the law. The police zoom to the scene of the crime with loud sirens and flashing lights. In an emergency, the police can drive very fast. Police cars can speed at 155 miles per hour (249 km/h)— twice as fast as a cheetah!

The police have plenty of jobs to do. They catch criminals, find lost or stolen things, and keep people safe. The police use all kinds of vehicles for their work. Motorcycles and cars get them to an emergency fast. But if the police need to keep an eye on a large area, they use a helicopter. Helicopters can hover in the sky like an insect, while the police look around.

Hey you, let me in! It's the police. There's been a robbery at the local gym.

Aha! It looks like I've caught you red-handed. What do you have to say for yourself?

Um, these are just my boxing gloves. They're only good for stealing last-minute knockouts . . .

Splash! A criminal thinks he can get away by zooming across the ocean in a speedboat. He's wrong! The police patrol the oceans, too. Police boats can reach speeds of 46 miles per hour (74 km/h), as fast as a shark. This boat also has a loudspeaker, "Hey, you! Stop! Police!"

BUILD IT!

There's a crime to fight on the high seas! Build a super-speedy police boat to help track down the criminals.

POLICE 14

Our big engines help us zip across the water. We are closing in on you, thief!

I've got a sinking feeling. Let's catch up later, OK?

I'm in charge of things under the sea. That crook is out of her depth!

Ocean heroes

The police aren't the only heroes making a splash on the ocean. If someone gets lost at sea, the coast guard is off to the rescue. Their boats and helicopters use special equipment called radar.

The coast guard carries out more than 100 rescue missions a day.

Can I be a coast guard, too? I'm a great swimmer and an expert in merm-aid.

Radar uses radio waves to find lost things, even deep in the ocean.

Ahoy, me hearties! My pirate ship is in a spot of trouble. I need a rescue!

Your ship isn't the ONLY thing in trouble. Is that a STOLEN treasure chest I can see?

This old chest? That's just where I keep my spare peg leg!

Hospital heroes

When someone is sick or injured, they need treatment fast. Woo woo woo! An ambulance races to the scene within minutes. It's like a hospital on wheels! And the paramedics at the wheel know just what to do.

An ambulance is packed with plenty of first-aid supplies to help fix people. What happened to you?

I tried to close a revolving door.

The paramedics work fast. They help out at the scene and then take people to a hospital if they need more care.

BUILD IT!

Build an ambulance able to dodge through traffic at top speeds. Don't forget to add flashing lights!

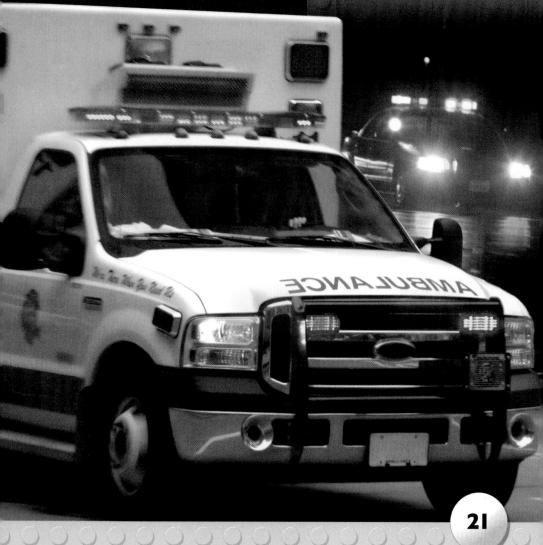

21

Ambulances can travel at more than 100 miles per hour (160 km/h), but sometimes that isn't fast enough. Vroom, Vroom! Paramedics on special motorcyles can travel at up to 141 miles per hour (255 km/h). They can squeeze in and out of traffic.

They can reach places that other ambulances can't. They carry enough equipment to save lives.

Oh no! Someone is injured. A regular ambulance would take hours to reach them. Who can help? Look up in the sky. It's an air ambulance. This helicopter can land in a space as small as a tennis court. In Australia, the Royal Flying Doctor Service uses air ambulances every day. They can reach patients who live hundreds of miles into the countryside.

Who needs my help? I've just landed in the front yard, and the hospital has a team waiting.

Excuse me, this is an AIR ambulance, not a BEAR ambulance! Sigh. I'll do my best to help.

Mountain rescue

Look at that view! But the weather changes quickly in the mountains. Steep paths twist and turn. Someone is lost. It's hard for a rescue team to find them. They need tough vehicles with big tires to grip the rocky ground.

Hey, you look lost! Let me help you. I know these mountains better than your GPS!

No thanks um, sir, I'm fine, really . . . Help! There's a monster chasing me!

It takes awesome pilot skills to move through the mountains. I'm on it!

A helicopter can help. It hovers in the air. Its crew lowers a rope to rescue people from tight spots. Good work, rescue team!

It's freezing today in the mountains. Snow is piled high. A skier is stranded! A snowmobile has skis of its own so it can glide over the snow. It has tracks at the back to grip the icy ground. Woof woof! The rescue dog will help, too. He is trained to sniff out people who are lost in the snow.

Good dog! The snowmobile has lifesaving equipment on board. Its driver can also speed hurt people off the mountain to get help.

Just dropping in to find out what you've learned.

BUILD IT!

Create a super-speedy snowmobile to race over the highest snowdrifts.

To the rescue!

It's another busy day for the minifigure emergency services. Use your stickers to show them rushing to the rescue. Don't forget helicopters flying high in the sky!

LICE LINE • DO NOT CROSS • POLICE LINE

Emergency words

Criminal
Somebody who
breaks the law.

Emergency
A serious problem
that needs to be
fixed right away.

Hover
To stay in one place
in the air.

(The) Law
A long list of rules that
everybody in a country
has to follow. Stealing
is against the law.

Nozzle
A round part at the end
of a hose that is used to
control how fast the
water sprays out.

Paramedic
A person who drives
an ambulance or
motorcycle and who
knows emergency
treatment but is
not a doctor.

Patient
A person who needs
help from a doctor,
nurse, or paramedic.

Patrol
To travel around an
area and check what
is happening there.

Radar
A machine that can
find boats and other
objects in the sea or
the sky. Airplanes
also have radar.

Stolen
Something that
has been taken
from someone
without asking.

DO NOT CROSS

Did you read this
book cover to cover?
You see, I'm an
undercover cop.

Index

Credits

A
air ambulance 24, 25
ambulance 20, 21, 22, 23, 24

B
boat 18

C
cheetah 12
coast guard 18
crime 17
criminal 13, 14, 16, 17, 31
crook 15, 17

D
dogs 6, 28, 29

E
emergency 4, 5, 12, 14, 15, 18, 30, 31
engines 17

F
fire 6, 7, 6, 9 ,10, 11
fire department 9
fire plane 10
fire station 6
fire truck/engine 6, 7, 8, 10
firefighters 4, 6, 8, 10
flames 6

GH
helicopter 13, 15, 18, 24, 25, 27, 30
helmet 7
heroes 4, 5, 18, 20
hoses 6, 8
hospital 20, 24
hover 14, 27

IJKL
ladder truck 8
ladders 8, 9
law 12, 31
loudspeaker 16

M
minifigures 8, 30
motorcycle 14, 22
mountains 26, 27, 28, 29

N
nozzles 6, 31

O
ocean 16, 18, 19
officers 13

PQ
paramedics 20, 21, 22, 31
patients 24
patrol 13, 16
patrol cars 13

pilots 10, 27
platform 8
police 5, 12, 13, 14, 15, 16, 18
police boat 16, 17
police cars 12, 13

R
radar 18, 19, 31
radio waves 19
ramp 13
rescue 4, 6, 18, 19, 26, 27, 30
robbery 14

S
sea 17, 18
siren 6, 12
skis 28
snowmobile 28, 29
speedboat 16
stolen 14, 19, 31

T
tanker fire trucks 7
thief 17
tires 26

UV
vehicles 4, 5, 14, 26

WXYZ
wildfire 10, 11

For the LEGO Group: Peter Moorby *Licensing Coordinator*; Heidi K. Jensen *Licensing Manager*; Paul Hansford *Creative Publishing Manager*; Martin Leighton Lindhardt *Publishing Graphic Designer*

Photos ©: cover top right: Travis Manley/Dreamstime; cover center: Robwilson39/Dreamstime; cover top border: nadla/iStockphoto; cover background: Iakov Kalinin/Dreamstime; 1 center: dan_prat/iStockphoto; 1 background: PhotoAlto/James Hardy/Getty Images; 2-3 background: ruig/iStockphoto; 3 plane: Alessandro Colle/Shutterstock, Inc.; 4-5 top background: Matthew Collingwood/Dreamstime; 4 boat: Natalia Bratslavsky/Dreamstime; 4 police SUV: Carso80/iStockphoto; 4-5 center background: Johannesk/Dreamstime; 4-5 fire engine: ryasick/iStockphoto; 5 helicopter: Maria Jeffs/Shutterstock, Inc.; 5 ambulance: DigtialStorm/iStockphoto; 6-7 background: Crystal Craig/Dreamstime; 7 fire engine: Donald R. Swartz/Shutterstock, Inc.; 7 fireman: Mike Brake/Shutterstock, Inc.; 8-9: David Traiforos/Dembinsky Photo Associates/Alamy Images; 10 background: BanksPhotos/Getty Images; 10-11 plane: Rick Pisio/RWP Photography/Alamy Images; 11 bottom fire: Lucian Coman/Dreamstime; 11 background: USFS Photo/Alamy Images; 12-13 top background: Fotomak/Dreamstime; 12-13 police tape: leonardo255/iStockphoto; 12-13 police car: Frogtravel/Dreamstime; 12-13 bottom background: Rouzes/iStockphoto; 14-15 background: Nam Nguyen/Dreamstime; 15 helicopter: Mb2006/Dreamstime; 15 searchlight: kevinjeon00/iStockphoto; 16-17 background: Kanate/Dreamstime; 16-17 boat: motive56/Shutterstock, Inc.; 18-19 main: Petty Officer 1st Class Jamie Thielen/US Coast Guard; 19 top right: Petty Officer 2nd Class Tara Molle/US Coast Guard; 20-21 background: VisionsofAmerica/Joe Sohm/Media Bakery; 20-21 ambulance: Bryant Jayme/Shutterstock, Inc.; 22-23 background: wonry/iStockphoto; 23 bike: one-image photography/Alamy Images; 24-25 background: robynmac/iStockphoto; 24-25 helicopter: imaginewithme/iStockphoto; 26-27 background: 4nadia/iStockphoto; 27 truck: Jim Parkin/Shutterstock, Inc.; 28-29 background: THEPALMER/iStockphoto; 28 dog: Nikolai Tsvetkov/Shutterstock, Inc.; 29 snowmobile: Cylonphoto/Dreamstime; 30-31 top: Phonlamai Photo/Shutterstock, Inc.; 30-31 center: Lyu Hu/Shutterstock, Inc.; 30-31 bottom: mexrix/Shutterstock, Inc.; 30-31 police tape: leonardo255/iStockphoto; 32 top background: Kanate/Dreamstime; 32 helicopter: Gary Crabbe/Alamy Images; 32 bottom background: Olivier Le Queinec/Dreamstime.

All LEGO® illustrations and stickers by Paul Lee.

> Thanks to all the minifigure heroes for saving the day. This book is over and out!